Eat Your Way to Happiness

Eat Your Way to Happiness

Flavor-Packed Recipes
to Help Drive Away the Blues

SIMON MELHUISH

BARNES & NOBLE
NEW YORK

INTRODUCTION

Lost your job? Honey left you? Repo man knocking at the door? Never mind! Give yourself a giant-sized lift with these delicious happy dishes from across the world. The flavor-packed recipes in the following pages will drive away the blues and have you singing like a lark! Here's a little "taster" of the delights to come...

Sunny Side Up

There's nothing like getting the day off to a good start, and in Chapter 1 you'll find a range of happy breakfast recipes to lift your mood in the morning and set you up for the rest of the day. From *Well-Rounded Cheese Omelets* to *Comforting Muffins With Zing*, these merry meals will brighten the grayest dawn—even if

it's a Monday, and you've got nothing but a tough meeting with the boss to look forward to...

Banishing the Blues

Later in the day you'll need something more substantial, and in this cheery chapter you'll find a range of warming, comforting meals—from *Heart-Warming Beef Stew* to *Pork with Mushrooms and Thyme*. Nothing's so bad it won't seem better after one of these filling repasts. As writer Arnold Lobel put it, "All's well that ends with a good meal!"

Feelin' Good

Here's a selection of happy, healthy dishes to put a spring in your step—the recipes range from *Sizzling Seafood Stir-Fry Special* to *Tangy Pasta in Gooey Cheese*, from *Summer-Sunshine Vegetables* to *Melt-in-the-Mouth Chicken Breasts*. See for yourself—even the names are bound to cheer you up. Just imagine what the meals will do!

Hello Sunshine

Finally, everyone loves a tasty dessert, so don't miss out! In Chapter 4 you'll find delectable sweet recipes guaranteed to put a satisfied grin on anyone's face. From *Tipsy Pineapple Treats* to *Granny's Nana Muffins*, *Marvelously Limey Meringue Pie* to *Polly's Peachy Tarts*, these feel-good desserts will put the sunshine back in anyone's life.

And there you have it! Amazing but true—you really can eat your way to happiness with these fantastic dishes! So why be glum, chum? The solution is in your own hands. Turn the page, choose your favorite recipe, and get cooking. Happiness will be yours just a few short steps later—guaranteed!

Start the day with
a good breakfast—
and the sun will
shine on you...

Chapter One

SUNNY SIDE UP

Breakfasts and Brunches to put a Smile on your Face

Whether you're a morning person or a night owl—you'll be wide awake after these happy meals...

CONTENTS

COMFORTING MUFFINS WITH ZING

THESE MUNCHY MUFFINS ARE A LITTLE BIT SPECIAL! SERVE THEM FOR BREAKFAST AND THAT "ZING" WILL BE WITH YOU ALL DAY LONG!

Makes 8

What to buy

* **2 oz all-purpose flour**
* **A pinch of salt**
* **1 tsp ground ginger**
* **1 tbsp baking powder**
* **2 oz uncooked oatmeal**
* **Grated zest and juice of ½ orange**
* **2 oz sugar**
* **1 small egg**
* **3 ½ oz butter, melted**
* **½ cup milk**

How to cook it...

1 Heat the oven to 425°F. Sift flour, salt, ginger, and baking powder into a bowl. Stir in the oats, zest, and sugar; make a well in the center. Briskly beat the egg, butter, and milk together, add the orange juice, and pour into the well. Stir to combine all the ingredients.

2 Spoon the mixture into a greased muffin pan and bake for 15-20 minutes, until risen and firm to the touch. After a few minutes, remove from the pan and leave to cool on a wire rack.

3 Serve with a mug of steamy hot coffee or a glass of tangy fruit juice.

The walk downstairs to the breakfast table is exercise enough for any gentleman... (C.M. De Pew)

Raring to go

Look at the following statements.

(a) I take ages to "come to" in the morning.

(b) Before I've had a cup of coffee and a cigarette I'm not worth talking to.

(c) I get stressed easily and shout at people.

If any—or all—of these describe you, this protein-packed dish could be the answer to your problems. It'll make you alert and ready to face the world.

Inexpensive

Here's a good reason to be happy: although smoked salmon has a reputation for being a luxury food, prices have in fact dropped, and for this dish you can even use trimmings, available at most supermarkets—perfect for guilt-free indulgence!

SUNSHINE EGGS WITH SMOKED SALMON

CELEBRATE THE START OF ANY DAY WITH SUNSHINE— GOLDEN SCRAMBLED EGGS AND CLASSY SMOKED SALMON.

Serves 4

What to buy

* ✳ 4 tbsp butter
* ✳ 8 eggs
* ✳ 4 tbsp heavy cream
* ✳ ½ tbsp prepared mustard
* ✳ 4 oz smoked salmon, roughly chopped
* ✳ 2 tbsp fresh parsley, chopped
* ✳ 2 tbsp fresh chives, snipped
* ✳ Salt and pepper
* ✳ 1 tsp fresh dill, chopped

How to cook it...

1 Heat the butter in a non-stick frying pan. In a bowl, whisk eggs and cream, then add to the pan. Cook for about 3 minutes, stirring, until the eggs begin to set.

2 Add the smoked salmon, parsley, mustard, and chives, and continue cooking for about 1–2 minutes, or until the eggs are done and the smoked salmon has become opaque. Season with salt and pepper to taste.

3 Transfer to serving plates and sprinkle with the dill. Serve with a Mimosa or neat Champagne on red-letter days.

Easy does it

These wraps are very easy to put together, and they give endless room for variations. Adapt to suit every member of the family—try a fishy filling with shrimp, wild mushrooms with garlic, or a mixed-bean salad.

Sunny Eggs

Modern research has shown that high-protein food, such as eggs, can produce a feeling of calm. They contain the amino acid tryptophan which, when digested, produces serotonin—a drug that acts on the brain's neurotransmitters. Low levels of serotonin have been linked to depression—high levels to happiness. Now isn't that just eggstraordinary??!

All happiness depends on a leisurely breakfast...
(John Gunther)
—so take this to heart!

WARMLY WRAPPED EGGS AND PEPPERS

IN TWO WORDS: FAN...TASTIC! THESE WRAPS WILL GUARANTEE A HAPPY BREAKFAST TIME.

Serves 4

What to buy

* ✳ 4 flour tortillas
* ✳ 4 eggs
* ✳ 4 tbsp heavy cream
* ✳ A pinch of salt
* ✳ 2 tsp butter
* ✳ I onion, chopped
* ✳ 4 thin slices of ham, cut into strips
* ✳ 2 red bell peppers, seeded and chopped
* ✳ I chili, seeded and chopped
* ✳ 4 tbsp sour cream

How to cook it...

1 Heat the oven to 350°F. Wrap tortillas in foil and warm in the oven for 10 minutes.

2 Meanwhile, lightly beat the eggs with the cream and salt. Melt the butter in a frying pan over medium heat. Add the onion and fry for 5 minutes until translucent. Add the ham, eggs, bell peppers, and chili. Reduce the heat a little and stir constantly, until the eggs are just beginning to set. Remove from heat.

3 Place each tortilla on a plate. Spread with sour cream. Spoon egg mixture into the center, fold, and serve with a tomato salad and a big smile on your face!

...a recipe is only a theme which an intelligent cook can play each time with a variation... (Anon)

Honey Magic

Transformed by bees from nectar in the sunny countries of the world, honey has a certain magic about it. In ancient times, it was considered the food of the gods. It was used as an offering to placate angry deities, and was generally considered a symbol of wealth and happiness.

Sweet 'n' healthy

If you crave something sweet when you feel a bit low, explore the "happy" option: honey is a natural source of concentrated sugar, containing minerals such as potassium, calcium, magnesium, and iron, as well as most B vitamins and vitamin C.

HONEY 'N' HAM TOASTS

A SWELL WAY TO START THE DAY—THE HONEY WILL BRING OUT THE BEST FLAVORS IN THE HAM, AND THE BEST MOOD IN YOUR HONEY!

Serves 4

What to buy

- ✳ **8 slices whole-wheat bread for toasting**
- ✳ **4 tbsp low-fat cream cheese**
- ✳ **4 tsp acacia or other honey**
- ✳ **4 tsp sun-dried tomato purée**
- ✳ **4 thin slices cooked Maryland or other cooked ham**

How to cook it...

1 Toast the bread in the toaster or under the grill, until golden brown on both sides. Spread the cream cheese on four of the slices and, with a spoon, drizzle the honey evenly over the top of the cheese toasts.

2 Spread the other four slices of toast with the tomato purée, then top each one with a slice of Maryland ham.

3 Serve the toasts, lean back, uncrease your brow, and listen to the morning broadcast on the radio, or peruse the papers for good news.

17

A good cook is like a sorceress who dispenses happiness...
(Elsa Schiaparelli)

Start the day well...

Nutritionists agree that a decent breakfast
is the best start of the day. And Feng Shui
followers will insist that you should eat something
hot in the morning. As well as giving you energy,
it staves off mid-morning cravings for unhealthy
snacks (chips, cookies...). This fry-up is a good
general pick-me-up if you're in the doldrums. After
all, an army marches on its stomach...

Meat-free Meals

For a vegetarian option,
leave out the bacon in
this fry-up, and replace
it with slices of
eggplant dipped in
beaten egg and
breadcrumbs.
Alternatively, use
vegetarian bacon or
sausages.

CHEER-UP AND FRY-UP

THIS MAGNIFICENT BREAKFAST FEAST SURE WILL GIVE YOU A GOOD ENERGY BOOST, SO YOU'LL BE READY FOR ANYTHING THE DAY'S GONNA THROW AT YOU...

Serves 4

What to buy

※ **4 tbsp vegetable oil**

※ **4 sausages**

※ **8 strips of bacon**

※ **4 tomatoes, halved**

※ **4 large open-cup mushrooms, sliced**

※ **1 large can baked beans**

※ **8 slices of bread for toasting**

How to cook it...

1 Heat the oil in a large frying pan. Place the sausages in the pan and reduce the heat. Gently fry the sausages for about 15–20 minutes, turning them occasionally.

2 Meanwhile, heat the grill. Place the bacon under the grill, turning it once, until nicely crisp.

3 After about 10 minutes, add the halved tomatoes and the mushroom slices to the sausage pan. In a saucepan, heat the baked beans. Toast the bread.

4 Serve with a healthy glass of orange or grapefruit juice, followed by a frothy latte or cappuccino.

WELL-ROUNDED CHEESE OMELETS

RISE AND SHINE WITH THESE ADORABLE OMELETS. A TASTE OF HEAVEN IN YOUR KITCHEN—AND OH SO PERFECTLY FORMED!

Serves 4

What to buy

* ✳ **3 beefsteak tomatoes**
* ✳ **2 tbsp butter**
* ✳ **4 eggs**
* ✳ **Salt and pepper**
* ✳ **A small handful of arugula**
* ✳ **3 oz goat cheese**

How to cook it...

1 Plunge the tomatoes in boiling water for about 1 minute, then slip off the skins. Quarter and seed the tomatoes, and dice the flesh. Melt 1 tbsp butter in a frying pan, add the tomatoes, and cook very gently over a low heat for about 5 minutes. Leave to cool.

2 In a bowl, beat the eggs and season to taste. Stir in the fried tomatoes.

3 Melt the remaining butter in a clean frying pan, add the egg and tomato mixture, and cook four omelets. Cook them in one or two batches at a time, depending on the size of the frying pan. Remove omelets once cooked and keep them warm in the oven, at a very low setting.

4 Transfer the omelets to individual warmed serving plates. Roughly tear the arugula and distribute evenly over the omelets, then crumble the goat cheese on top.

5 Serve with crusty bread to mop up the juices—enjoy this moment of happiness: these plates won't need washing up!

Many's the night I've dreamed of cheese—toasted mostly... (Ben Gunn, Treasure Island)

Happy Goats

The goat cheese on these omelets won't melt. Instead it will just soften and ooze in the most tantalizing fashion. If you're not keen on the tart, zesty flavor of goat cheese, don't miss out on these fantastic breakfast omelets. Just substitute your favorite hard cheese made from cows' milk, and be happy!

Miracle chocolate

In France, in the 18th century, chocolate was widely considered a wonder drug. Medicinal chocolate was available to cure all sorts of ills, ranging from a cough to swelling. The "must-have" brand was Debauve, named for the pharmacist to King Louis XVI. Even today, chocoholics the world over make miracle claims for this special substance. And who are we to doubt them?

Keep them fresh

Muffins are best eaten on the day they're made—and they usually are! However, if you have made a large number of muffins, wait till they have cooled completely, then freeze for up to three months in a freezer bag.

Research tells us that 14 out of 10 individuals like chocolate... (Anon)

CHEERY CHOCOLATE MUFFINS

WHAT A TREAT FIRST THING IN THE MORNING! THESE CHUNKY, CHOCOLATEY MUFFINS ARE JUST WHAT THE DOCTOR ORDERED!

Makes 12

What to buy

* 1 lb all-purpose flour
* 2 tbsp unsweetened cocoa
* 1/2 tsp baking soda
* 1 tbsp baking powder
* 6 tbsp soft brown sugar
* 1/2 tsp ground allspice
* 1/2 tsp ground cinnamon
* 2 oz dark chocolate
* Grated zest of 1 orange
* 1 egg
* 1 cup milk

How to cook it...

1 Heat the oven to 400°F. Place the flour, cocoa, baking soda, baking powder, brown sugar, and allspice in a bowl. Break the chocolate into pieces and stir it into the bowl, together with the orange zest. Beat the egg and milk together, then fold into the dry ingredients.

2 Spoon the mixture into 12 muffin cups. Bake in the oven for about 15 minutes, or until risen and firm to the touch.

3 Serve and make sure you get some for yourself before they're all gone!

SMILEY CRÊPES

SPREAD A LITTLE HAPPINESS WITH THESE HONEY-SWEET CONFECTIONS. SERVE THEM AT BREAKFAST TO ENSURE EVERYONE STARTS THE DAY WITH A SMILE!

Makes 12

What to buy

* 4 oz all-purpose flour
* 4 oz sugar
* A pinch of salt
* 1 tsp baking powder
* 2 eggs
* 1 cup milk
* 2 tbsp butter, melted
* Warmed strawberry jam
* Lemon juice and honey to serve

How to cook it...

1 In a large bowl, combine the flour, sugar, salt, and baking powder. Make a well in the center and crack in the eggs.

2 Whisk the dry ingredients together with the eggs, then start adding the milk, a little at a time. Whisk until the batter is smooth. Add the melted butter and whisk.

3 Grease the bottom of a frying pan and heat. Working in batches, pour about 4 tbsp of the batter into the pan for each crêpe. Cook until the top is bubbly and the crêpe is dry around the edges. Carefully lift up with a slotted spoon or spatula, then flip over the crêpes and cook the second side until golden.

4 Put the strawberry jam into a piping bag and pipe smiley faces and a happy "good morning" message onto the crêpes. Alternatively, use a small spoon to drizzle a pattern on the crêpes. Serve with plenty of honey and lemon—and, of course, a big smile.

Never work before breakfast; if you have to work before breakfast, eat your breakfast first... (Josh Billings)

Warm Smiles

If, for some reason, you cannot eat all your crêpes in one go, you can keep them warm for a short time and prolong the happiness. Place the crêpes on a large plate and cover with foil, and then put the plate on top of a pan of simmering water.

GOOD-MORNING POPPY ROLLS

THERE'S NOTHING QUITE LIKE THE SMELL OF FRESHLY BAKED BREAD AND FRESHLY BREWED COFFEE—MORNINGS WERE MADE FOR THIS!

Makes 12

What to buy

* 2 oz butter
* 1 tbsp superfine granulated sugar
* 1 cup milk
* 1 lb 2 oz white heavy flour
* 1 ½ tsp salt
* 2 tsp dried yeast
* 2 eggs
* 2 tbsp milk
* 4 tsp poppy seeds

How to cook it...

1 Heat the oven to 400°F. In a saucepan, heat the butter, sugar, and milk until the butter has melted and the sugar has dissolved. Cool until tepid.

2 Sift the flour and salt into a bowl, stir in the yeast, and make a well in the center. Beat the eggs, reserve 1 tbsp of the mixture, and add the rest with the milk mixture to the dry ingredients. Mix to form a soft dough.

3 Knead the dough on a floured surface until smooth and elastic. Wrap in oiled plastic wrap, and leave to rise in a warm place for 1 hour, or until doubled in size.

4 Knead again, then divide into 12 even-sized rolls. Place onto a greased baking sheet, cover, and leave to rise for about 30 minutes, or until they have doubled in size.

5 Mix the reserved beaten egg with the milk and brush the rolls with this mixture. Sprinkle with poppy seeds. Bake in the oven for about 20 minutes, or until golden.

6 Place on a wire rack to cool a little, then call everyone to breakfast—if they're not eagerly sitting at the table already!

> Without bread
> all is misery...
> (William Cobbett)

Happy Noses

Smells have a major effect on our well-being, and freshly baked bread is one of the strongest feel-good smells. Marketing departments of supermarkets know this and spray artificial baked-bread scents around the store. Apparently, prospective house buyers are also more likely to sign a deal when they smell fresh bread!

Warming, comforting, blissfully indulgent—the best type of food to make you feel happy again...

Chapter Two

BANISHING THE BLUES

Home-Style Cookin'—When You're Feelin' Lonesome and Blue

29

Cook yourself a treat, curl up on the sofa, and don't worry—be happy!

CONTENTS

CHICKEN SOUP FOR THE SOUL

WHEN IT'S COLD OUTSIDE YOU'LL BE GLOWING INSIDE WITH A BOWL OF THIS WINTER WARMER INSIDE YOU. SOUP-ERB!

Serves 4

What to buy

* ✳ 4 chicken pieces
* ✳ 1 small parsnip, chopped
* ✳ 1 turnip, halved
* ✳ ½ rutabaga, chopped
* ✳ 1 bay leaf
* ✳ 10 peppercorns
* ✳ 1 large onion, chopped
* ✳ 2 garlic cloves
* ✳ 4 sticks celery, sliced
* ✳ 2 carrots, sliced
* ✳ 2 leeks, cut into rings
* ✳ Salt and pepper
* ✳ 4 oz vermicelli noodles

How to cook it...

1 Put the chicken in a large saucepan. Add the parsnip, turnip, rutabaga, and the spices. Cover with cold water and bring to a boil. Turn down the heat, cover, and simmer gently for about 30 minutes. After 10 minutes, skim off any fat.

2 Remove the vegetables with a slotted spoon, squeeze out any juices, and discard. Add the remaining vegetables and simmer for another 30 minutes until they are tender. Season to taste.

3 Add the vermicelli noodles and simmer for 5 minutes or until the noodles are soft.

4 Serve piping hot, and remember how Mom used to comfort you: "There, there, it's all better now, isn't it?"

Pasta for Pleasure

Not only is pasta the perfect comfort food, it's also one of the healthiest. Like rice and potatoes, it's an excellent source of complex carbohydrates, which, nutritionists agree, we need to stay in tip-top shape.

La Dolce Vita

In need of a quick and easy pick-me-up? Then reach for the pasta, and turn that frown upside-down! As you tuck into this soothing dish of tagliatelle with its sinfully rich creamy sauce, allow your mind to transport you to sunsets on the Italian Riviera, or to romantic candlelit dinners for two at your favorite local restaurant. Before you know it, your problems will seem so far away...

Kissing don't last: cookery do! (George Meredith)

CREAMY TAGLIATELLE

THIS LUXURIOUSLY CREAMY DISH IS THE PERFECT PICK-ME-UP PASTA, GREAT FOR CHASING AWAY WINTER GLOOM ON COLD, DARK NIGHTS.

Serves 4

What to buy

* 1 lb tagliatelle or fettucine
* 3 egg yolks
* 1 ½ fl oz heavy cream
* 2 ½ oz hard cheese (for example Pecorino or Parmesan), grated
* A pinch of nutmeg
* Salt and pepper
* A pinch of paprika
* 1 tbsp butter

How to cook it...

1 Cook the pasta in plenty of salted water until firm to the bite. Meanwhile, beat the egg yolks and cream together in a mixing bowl. Add the cheese and all the seasonings.

2 Melt the butter in a frying pan over a low heat. Add the hot noodles and stir until coated with butter. Season to taste and add the egg-cream mixture. Mix quickly over low heat until all the pasta is well-coated.

3 Serve in front of the fireplace—and purr like the cat that's gotten the cream.

HEART-WARMING BEEF STEW

WHEN YOU FEEL REALLY DOWN, THIS SATISFYING CASSEROLE WILL CHEER YOU UP—BUT YOU COULD ALWAYS ADD A SPLASH OF BEER FOR EXTRA BLISS!

Serves 4

What to buy

* **3 tbsp vegetable oil**
* **1 3/4 lb beef, chuck or brisket, trimmed and cut into bite-size pieces**
* **4 onions, roughly chopped**
* **12 oz carrots, cut into chunks**
* **2 tbsp all-purpose flour**
* **20 fl oz fresh beef stock**
* **1 tbsp tomato purée**
* **1 bay leaf**
* **Salt and pepper**

How to cook it...

1 Heat the oven to 325°F. In a large ovenproof casserole dish, heat the oil. Add the beef and brown in batches, stirring. Remove the meat with a slotted spoon and set aside.

2 Reduce the heat, add the onions and carrots to the casserole, and sauté for about 5 minutes, or until they are lightly browned. Sprinkle over the flour, stir, and cook for about 2 minutes.

3 Gradually add the beef stock, stir in the tomato purée, and add the bay leaf. Season generously. Return the meat with all the juices that have collected back to the casserole. Bring slowly to a boil.

4 Cover the casserole and cook in the oven for about 1 ½ hours, or until the meat is tender. Check occasionally and add a little water or more stock if the stew becomes too dry.
5 Serve the stew piping hot, with mashed potatoes, rice, or dumplings—and watch the world turn a glowing shade of pink.

The perfect recipe for the days when you feel life's getting you in a stew!

Dumpling Stew

Home-made dumplings will increase the happiness quotient: For 8 small ones, put 4 oz self-rising flour in a bowl and season. Stir in 2 oz lard and ¼ tsp fresh chopped herbs, then add just enough water to make a soft dough. Shape into 8 dumplings and add to the stew, about 25–30 minutes before it's due to be ready. Enjoy!

CHEESY BROCCOLI GRATIN

WHEN THE WIND IS HOWLING AND THE RAIN POUNDING THE ROOF, FLOAT AWAY TO SUNNIER CLIMES WITH THIS DISH OF CREAMY DELIGHT.

Serves 4

What to buy

* 9 oz new potatoes
* 1 lb broccoli
* 1 tbsp vegetable oil
* 2 red onions, chopped
* 1 red bell pepper, seeded and chopped
* 5 oz cheddar cheese, grated
* 2 9 oz tubs of soft cream cheese
* 1 tbsp cornstarch mixed with 1 tbsp water
* 1 tbsp fresh parsley, chopped
* Salt and pepper
* A handful of fresh white breadcrumbs

How to cook it...

1 Heat the oven to 400°F. Cut the vegetables into chunks of roughly the same size. In a large saucepan, boil the potatoes in salted water for 5 minutes. Add the broccoli and cook for a further 5 minutes. Drain well and put in a buttered ovenproof dish.

2 Heat the oil in a saucepan and gently cook the onions and pepper for about 5 minutes until they're soft. Add them to the other vegetables in the ovenproof dish.

3 In a saucepan, heat half the grated cheese and the cream cheese. Once they've melted, stir in the blended cornstarch to thicken the mixture. Stir in the parsley, season to taste with salt and pepper, and then pour over the prepared vegetables.

4 Sprinkle everything with the breadcrumbs and the remaining cheese. Pop the dish into the preheated oven and bake for about 20 minutes, or until golden brown on top.

5 Now snuggle back on to the sofa and enjoy your heart-warming gratin.

Never eat anything at one sitting that you can't lift... (Miss Piggy)

Say "Cheese"

The simple pleasures of eating cheese take on a rather more serious guise in France, where so many varieties are produced you can eat a different one every day of the year. Charles de Gaulle is reported to have complained about the difficulty of running a country with more than 300 cheeses!

I never see any home cooking. All I get is fancy stuff...
(Prince Philip)

Buried Treasure

Potatoes are the ultimate comfort food, and with so many delicious ways to cook them, one's passion need never be spent. Think of them roasted, or baked to a crisp on the outside and melting within, or mashed into a fluffy pile. And if you're feeling in a particularly indulgent mood, remember, there's no end to the butter and cream that potatoes will mop up. There! Better now?

Mash with panache

Delectable as they are, plain mashed potatoes can easily be pepped up. Try adding some grated cheese or chopped scallions, or some sour cream and chives. Mustard and crème fraîche taste great with sausages and mash.

38

SAUSAGE AND MASH

ALLOW YOURSELF TO BE A KID AGAIN—THIS ALL-TIME CHILDREN'S FAVORITE ALSO GOES DOWN A TREAT WITH ADULTS!

Serves 4

What to buy

* 2 lbs potatoes
* 1 tbsp butter
* Salt and pepper
* A pinch of grated nutmeg
* 5 fl oz sour cream or yogurt
* 4 tbsp oil
* 8 spicy sausages

How to cook it...

1 Boil the potatoes until cooked, and drain. Add the butter, salt, nutmeg, and sour cream or yogurt, and mash. Set aside and keep warm.

2 Meanwhile, heat the oil in a frying pan. Add the sausages and sauté gently over a low heat, for about 10 minutes, turning occasionally. Transfer to serving plates. Add a little hot water and a splash of red wine to the pan and loosen the crispy bits with a spoon. Season to taste and spoon over the mash.

3 Take your place at the table—and think about happy moments in your childhood.

NICELY NUTTY CHICKEN CURRY

DREAM OF COCONUT PALM TREES ON FAR-AWAY SHORES—
AND THINGS WILL LOOK UP BEFORE YOU KNOW IT.

Serves 4

What to buy

* ✳ 2 tbsp vegetable oil
* ✳ 1 onion, chopped
* ✳ 2 garlic cloves, crushed
* ✳ 1 tbsp all-purpose flour
* ✳ 1 tsp ground ginger
* ✳ 1 tsp ground cumin
* ✳ 4 chicken breasts, skinned and cut into strips
* ✳ 4 oz unsalted cashew nuts
* ✳ 3 oz creamed coconut
* ✳ 20 fl oz chicken or vegetable stock
* ✳ 3 oz fresh coconut, finely grated
* ✳ 4 cardamom seeds
* ✳ A cinnamon stick
* ✳ Salt and pepper
* ✳ 1 mango, peeled and chopped

How to cook it...

1 Heat the oven to 300°F. Heat half the oil in a large flameproof casserole dish and gently fry the onion and garlic until soft. Add the flour, ginger, and cumin, stir, and cook for another 2 minutes. Set aside.

2 Meanwhile, heat the remaining oil in a frying pan. Sauté the chicken for about 5 minutes, until lightly browned, then add the cashew nuts.

3 Slowly pour the creamed coconut and the stock into the casserole, stirring constantly.

Add the grated coconut, chicken, cashew nuts, cardamom, and cinnamon, season to taste, cover, and cook in the oven for 30 minutes.
4 Add the mango, stir thoroughly, and return to the oven for a further 30 minutes.
5 Serve piping hot with steamed rice, and enjoy a taste of the totally tropical!

Mangoes are best eaten in the bathtub...
(Folk Wisdom)

Hindu Wisdom

In Hindu teaching, the mango is referred to as the "fruit of heavenly joy." That's because it's believed to contain natural chemicals that are closely related to modern-day anti-depressants. It's served here in a nutty chicken dish, but you can, of course, enjoy mango on its own, with ice cream, as part of a tropical fruit salad, or puréed.

FANTASTIC FISHERMAN'S PIE

EVEN IF YOU'RE ALL AT SEA, THIS HEARTWARMING PIE WILL RAISE YOUR SPIRITS AND SEND YOU OFF "FULL STEAM AHEAD"!

Serves 4

What to buy

* ✳ 10 oz potatoes, cut into chunks
* ✳ 10 oz parsnips, cut into chunks
* ✳ 2 ¼ lb haddock fillet, skinned
* ✳ 2 tbsp all-purpose flour
* ✳ Salt and pepper
* ✳ 2 tbsp vegetable oil
* ✳ 1 oz butter
* ✳ 3 fl oz milk
* ✳ 2 tbsp fresh parsley, chopped
* ✳ 2 oz cheddar cheese, grated

How to cook it...

1 Heat oven to 375°F. Cook the potatoes and parsnips in salted water for about 15 minutes, or until tender.

2 Meanwhile, cut the haddock fillet into short strips. Put the flour on a plate, and season with salt and pepper. Turn the fish in the flour until completely coated, then gently shake off any excess. Heat the oil in a frying pan and cook the strips of fish until golden brown. Transfer to a lightly greased ovenproof dish.

3 Drain the potatoes and parsnips. Mash them together with the butter, milk, and parsley. Season to taste. Spread the purée evenly over the fish, then sprinkle with the cheese.

4 Bake in the oven for 15–20 minutes, or until the cheese has melted. Everyone will love this culinary equivalent of a security blanket!

After a good dinner one can forgive anybody, even one's own relatives... (Oscar Wilde)

Catch of the day

You can use just about any white fish you have at hand for this warming and satisfying pie and it will taste every bit as good. But whether you opt for cheaper alternatives like whiting, or the more expensive cod, make sure that the fish is skinned and bone-free.

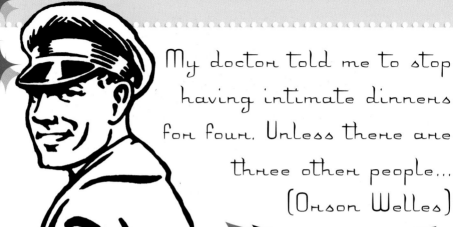

My doctor told me to stop having intimate dinners for four. Unless there are three other people...
(Orson Welles)

Praise for the Pig

Happily, maximum pleasure comes from minimum fuss where pork is concerned. The richness and succulence of the meat make it perfect for hearty, rustic cusine, like a simple, homely bacon sandwich or a gloriously crisp piece of roast crackling. It's also a relatively fatty meat, so accompaniments are best kept uncomplicated (and that sounds like a good excuse for an easy meal!).

A Taste of France

Normandy is justly proud of its local produce: pork, cream, and apples. The apples, especially, lead to much Norman happiness— they form the basis for magnificent ciders and apple brandies such as Calvados!

44

PORK WITH MUSHROOMS AND THYME

THIS FLAVOR-PACKED FRENCH RECIPE WILL DRIVE AWAY THE BLUES AND BRING THE SUNSHINE BACK TO YOUR LIFE. MAGNIFIQUE!

Serves 4

What to buy

* ✻ **4 boneless pork loin chops**
* ✻ **I oz butter**
* ✻ **6 oz button mushrooms, sliced**
* ✻ **2 tbsp fresh thyme, chopped**
* ✻ **2 tbsp light cream**
* ✻ **I tsp cornstarch, blended with I tbsp cider**
* ✻ **Salt and pepper**

How to cook it...

1 Melt the butter in a large frying pan. Fry the chops for about 6-8 minutes, turning once, or until golden brown all over.

2 Add the mushrooms and thyme to the pan and cook for a further 2-3 minutes.

3 Stir in the cream and cornstarch, and season to taste. Cook for another minute.

4 Serve with a large glass of cider—or apple brandy!—for extra comfort.

Mild 'n' Mellow Drinks

BANANA SMOOTHIE

SHARE A SMOOTHIE WITH A FRIEND AND LET IT TRANSPORT YOU INTO
A CHEERFUL STATE OF UNBRIDLED BLISS.

Serves 2

What to buy

※ **2 bananas, peeled and chopped**
※ **1 tray of ice cubes**
※ **½ pint light cream**
※ **2 tbsp honey**
※ **A pinch of cinnamon**

How to make it...

1 Place the bananas in a blender and whizz for 30 seconds. Add the ice, cream, and honey. Put the lid back on and pulse the blender a couple of times to break up the ice before whizzing up to a slushy milkshake consistency.

2 Transfer into two large glasses and sprinkle with the cinnamon.

3 Sit back and enjoy your smoothie with a satisfying slurp.

Mild 'n' Mellow Drinks
CAFÉ BRÛLOT
LET THE GOOD TIMES ROLL—AND ENJOY THIS CHEERY NEW ORLEANS SPECIAL.

Serves 2
What to buy

- ✳ 3 fl oz brandy
- ✳ 2 tbsp sugar
- ✳ Zest of 1 orange
- ✳ 2 cinnamon sticks
- ✳ 8 whole cloves
- ✳ 2 cups hot strong black coffee

How to make it...

1 Place the brandy, sugar, zest, and spices into a fireproof bowl and heat gently. When the mixture has heated through, take it off the stove and carefully ignite it with a match.

2 Allow to burn for a couple of minutes, then pour the hot coffee into the flaming brandy, and ladle everything into brûlot or espresso cups.

3 As you sit and sip your cocktail, dream up an outfit for the Mardi Gras parade!

Drunkenness is nothing but voluntary madness... (Seneca)

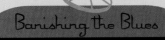

Mild 'n' Mellow Drinks
WEEP NO MORE
DOWN ONE OF THESE AND WIPE THEM TEARS AWAY!

Serves 2

What to buy

* 4 parts red Dubonnet
* 3 parts brandy
* 1 tsp maraschino cherry liqueur
* 2 parts fresh lime juice
* Crushed ice cubes

How to make it...

1 Put all the ingredients and the crushed ice cubes into the shaker and shake vigorously.
2 Pour into two well-chilled cocktail glasses and then down in one gulp—cheers!

Mild 'n' Mellow Drinks
SOUL KISS
WHEN YOU'VE GOT THE BIG CITY BLUES, AND YOU'VE GOT IT BAD— LET THIS COCKTAIL "KISS" YOU BETTER.

Serves 2

What to buy

※ **4 parts bourbon**
※ **2 parts dry vermouth**
※ **I part red Dubonnet**
※ **I part fresh orange juice**
※ **Crushed ice cubes**

How to make it...

1 Put all the ingredients, as well as plenty of crushed ice cubes, into the cocktail shaker and shake vigorously.
2 Pour into two well-chilled cocktail glasses. Now sit back, light a candle, and savor, as you listen to a few of your favorite tunes.

I'm not under the alkafluence of inkahol that some thinkle peep I am... (Harald Metz)

The Romans knew it already: a healthy (and happy) mind lives in a healthy body...

Chapter Three

FEELIN' GOOD

Fulsome Fare for Body and Soul

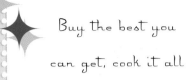

Buy the best you can get, cook it all yourself, and your body will thank you forever!

CONTENTS

SIZZLING SEAFOOD STIR-FRY SPECIAL

CHINESE MAGIC! THIS DELICIOUS, QUICK-AND-EASY STIR-FRY WILL MAKE THE WORLD SEEM A BETTER, BRIGHTER PLACE.

Serves 4

What to buy

* 5 oz rice noodles
* 3 tbsp vegetable oil
* 1-inch cube of fresh ginger, sliced
* 8 scallions, chopped
* 3 garlic cloves, crushed
* 9 oz mixed seafood (including shrimp, mussels, squid)
* 1 tbsp dry sherry
* 1 tbsp dark soy sauce
* 1 tbsp black bean sauce

How to cook it...

1 Place the rice noodles into a saucepan of boiling water and cook for about 3 minutes, or until just tender. Drain and keep warm.

2 Heat the oil in a large saucepan and add the ginger, scallions, garlic, and mixed seafood. Stir on a high heat for about 1 minute.

3 Stir in the sherry, soy sauce, 3 tbsp water, and black bean sauce. Cook for a further 2 minutes, add the noodles, and stir together to heat through.

4 Serve straight from the pan.

MELT-IN-THE-MOUTH CHICKEN BREASTS

THESE SUCCULENT STUFFED CHICKEN BREASTS WITH A MEDITERRANEAN FLAVOR ARE JUST DIVINE, AND SO HEALTHY, TOO!

Serves 4

What to buy

- ✳ **3 large red bell peppers**
- ✳ **10 sun-dried tomatoes in oil, coarsely chopped**
- ✳ **4 oz soft goat cheese**
- ✳ **4 boneless chicken breasts**
- ✳ **5 tbsp olive oil**
- ✳ **2 tbsp fresh rosemary, chopped**

How to cook it...

1 Heat the oven to 400°F. Holding the peppers with a long fork, roast them over a flame until the skins blacken. Place them in a plastic bag and close tight. After about 10 minutes remove, and peel off the skins. Slice the bell pepper flesh into strips and set aside.

2 In a bowl, combine the dried tomatoes, goat cheese, and roasted bell pepper strips. Mix well. Make several horizontal slits in each chicken breast and press in the mixture. Brush each breast with olive oil.

3 Place the chicken breasts on a grill over a roasting pan, and sprinkle over with the rosemary. Bake for about 30 minutes in the oven, or until the skins are crispy, and the juices run clear when you pierce the meat with a sharp knife.

4 Serve the chicken with a glass of light red or crisp white wine, and you'll start singing of happy days on southern shores.

The average American eats over 80 pounds of chicken each year.

Happy Sun

This combination of flavors is typical of the Mediterranean—olive oil predominates over saturated fats, in salad dressings and for cooking in general. Exciting research has shown that this diet is one of the healthiest in the world—life expectancy is high and the incidence rates of long-term diseases are low.

TERRIFIC TABBOULEH

THIS TANGY LEBANESE DISH IS THE PERFECT LUNCHTIME LIFTER. YOU'LL BE GRINNING ALL THROUGH THE AFTERNOON!

Serves 4

What to buy

* 4 tbsp fresh lemon juice
* 2 tbsp white wine vinegar
* 1 1/2 tsp dijon mustard
* 6 tbsp olive oil
* 1/2 tsp sugar
* 1/2 tsp ground cumin
* 8 oz couscous
* Zest and juice of 1 orange
* A handful of raisins
* A small handful of fresh mint, chopped
* A large handful of fresh parsley, chopped
* 4 scallions, chopped
* 2 stalks celery, chopped
* Salt and pepper
* A handful of mixed nuts (hazel or cashew), chopped

How to cook it...

1 Make a dressing: in a small bowl, whisk together the lemon juice, vinegar, mustard, oil, sugar, and cumin.

2 Place the couscous in a bowl, add 2 cups boiling water, or follow package directions, and leave to stand for 30–45 minutes, until it is light and fluffy. Drain and put in a bowl. Add 2 tbsp of the dressing; toss well.

3 Put the orange juice and the raisins in a small bowl and warm in a microwave. Leave to soak for about 15 minutes.

4 Add raisins, juice, zest, mint, parsley, scallions, celery, and the remaining dressing. Stir to mix and season to taste.

5 Just before serving, stir in the nuts, or pack them for the lunchbox. And don't forget a fork!

As for...mint, the very smell of it alone recovers and refreshes our spirits, as the taste stirs up our appetite...
(Pliny)

Best Grains

You can use couscous or the more traditional bulgur for this recipe. Couscous is made from durum wheat; bulgur is made by cooking the wheat, then drying the grains and cracking them. In fact, you'll sometimes see bulgur sold as cracked wheat.

Which Soy?

Soy sauce is one of the most popular sauces in the world, and has been used in Asia for centuries. For a subtly different effect, experiment with the vast range of Japanese, Chinese, and Indonesian soy sauces available in the shops. They're all slightly different, but, as a rule of thumb, the darker the color of the sauce, the more intense its flavor.

Meat and Fruit

Many dishes in East and West combine meat and fruit—just think of serving cranberries with turkey and venison, or apple sauce with pork. In this Far-Eastern recipe, the mango adds sweetness and the lime tartness.

The discovery of a new dish does more for the happiness of the human race than the discovery of a star...
(A. Brillat-Savarin)

TAKE-IT-EASY THAI SALAD

THIS JUICY, FRUITY STEAK SALAD IS THE PERFECT CHOICE FOR A LAID-BACK LUNCH. IT'S SIMPLY THAI-RRIFIC!

Serves 4

What to buy

- ✳ **8 oz filet mignon or boneless sirloin steak**
- ✳ **Vegetable oil, for brushing**
- ✳ **I ripe mango**
- ✳ **½ cucumber**
- ✳ **Zest and juice of I lime**
- ✳ **2 tbsp soy sauce**
- ✳ **I small red chili, thinly sliced**
- ✳ **2 tbsp fresh cilantro, chopped**
- ✳ **A small bunch of scallions, sliced**

How to cook it...

1 Heat a frying pan until very hot. Brush the steaks with the oil and fry for a minute or two on each side. Remove steaks from the pan and leave to cool.

2 Meanwhile, peel and thinly slice the mango and put in a bowl. Grate the cucumber and place in the bowl with the lime zest and juice, soy sauce, and chili.

3 Slice the steaks into thin strips and toss them well in the mango mixture.

4 Divide the steak salad between four serving plates and sprinkle with the cilantro and scallions.

5 Serve as a cold main course—and take it easy!

Ruling a large kingdom is like cooking a small fish—handle gently and never overdo it...

(Lao Tse)

Good for You

Fatty fish like salmon are full of omega-3 fatty acids, which boost the body's high-density lipoproteins. These are important in the fight against heart disease. Other fish with this magical property are mackerel, herring, and tuna. Eat as much of them as you can—at least twice a week. They'll keep you healthy and happy!

Star Spice

Within the pretty eight-pointed star of star anise are seeds with a slightly hot licorice flavor. They make up part of the Chinese five-spice powder, and the seeds are often chewed as a breath freshener.

Feelin' Good

SALMON IN A SOOTHING MARINADE

SALMON IS SUCH A SUPER FISH—ALWAYS TASTY, ELEGANT, AND YET SO LIGHT AND HEALTHY! WHAT MORE COULD YOU ASK FOR?

Serves 4

What to buy

✳ 2 tbsp soy sauce

✳ 4 tbsp dry sherry

✳ I red chili, chopped

✳ A piece of fresh ginger, finely diced

✳ I garlic clove, crushed

✳ 6 star anise, crushed

✳ 2 tbsp fresh cilantro, chopped

✳ I large salmon fillet, about I lb, cut into four portions

How to cook it...

1 Make the marinade: in a shallow bowl combine the soy sauce, sherry, chili, ginger, garlic, and star anise. Add the salmon and turn to coat with the marinade. Chill for at least 2 hours for the flavors to mingle.

2 When you are ready to cook, lift the fish out of the marinade and pat dry with paper towels. Heat a frying pan, and sear the salmon on both sides for about 2 minutes. Sprinkle the cilantro over the top.

3 Spoil yourself, and make this a really special meal: serve with wild rice, roasted fennel, and a glass of dry sherry or chilled Chardonnay.

Garlic is as good as ten mothers...

(Les Blank)

Pest or Pesto?

Italian pesto is bottled sunshine—and happiness—and one of the very best uses of the herb basil. For a quick and healthy meal, toss some hot pasta in a few tablespoons of pesto and smother with Parmesan cheese. You'll find it hard to believe that this king of herbs was once relegated to the bedroom—for deterring flies!

Super Food

Garlic, best known as anti-vampire insurance, has also warded off colds for centuries. Happily, recent research has found it to be a powerful anti-cancer food too, especially when taken together with sunshine and wine!

SUMMER-SUNSHINE VEGETABLES

THIS COLORFUL RICE DISH SINGS OF MEDITERRANEAN SUNSHINE
AND ITALIAN BEACHES—A BOOST FOR BODY AND SOUL AT ANY TIME.

Serves 4

What to buy

* 2 red bell peppers
* 2 yellow bell peppers
* I large eggplant
* 2 red onions
* 3 large zucchini
* 6 garlic cloves
* 3 tbsp olive oil
* 5 oz rice
* 5 fl oz hot vegetable stock
* 2-3 tbsp fresh pesto
* Fresh basil leaves, to garnish

How to cook it...

1 Heat the oven to 425°F. Trim and seed the vegetables, then cut them into chunks. Place them in a large roasting pan and drizzle with the oil. Toss well. Season and roast for about 20-30 minutes, or until the vegetables are tender.

2 Cook the rice according to manufacturer's instructions. Fluff with a fork.

3 Put the rice into a warmed serving dish. Spoon over the vegetables, drizzle with fresh pesto, and scatter with basil leaves.

4 Enjoy the sunshine taste of *la dolce vita* in your own home.

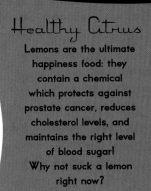

Healthy Citrus

Lemons are the ultimate happiness food: they contain a chemical which protects against prostate cancer, reduces cholesterol levels, and maintains the right level of blood sugar! Why not suck a lemon right now?

Saucy Pasta

Spaghetti, linguine, and vermicelli hold and distribute sauce extremely well. No matter what quantity of pasta you're cooking, always use a large pan with plenty of boiling water—that way, your pasta will never come to a sticky end.

Pasta and cheese —a marriage made in heaven... (Anon)

TANGY PASTA IN GOOEY CHEESE

SEND YOUR TASTE BUDS ON AN ITALIAN HOLIDAY—WITH THIS SUPER-FASTA PASTA RECIPE.

Serves 4

What to buy

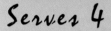

* 1 lb dried linguine or other pasta shapes
* Juice of 2 lemons
* 1/3 cup olive oil
* 4 1/2 oz Parmesan, freshly grated
* 2 handfuls of fresh basil, chopped
* 1 handful of arugula

How to cook it...

1 Cook the linguine according to manufacturer's instructions in plenty of boiling salted water, then drain and return to the saucepan.

2 Meanwhile, beat the lemon juice with the olive oil, then stir in the Parmesan until thick and creamy. Season generously and add more lemon juice if desired.

3 Add the sauce to the linguine and shake the pan to coat each strand of pasta. The Parmesan melts when mixed with the pasta. Stir in the basil and arugula.

4 Serve this mouthwatering dish with plenty of crusty bread and a fresh tomato salad.

Be Prepared

Happiness is a well-prepared barbecue with no last-minute hitches. You can make these lamburgers in advance and keep them in the refrigerator for a few hours until you're ready to cook them. Just prepare them to the end of step 2. And if the weather doesn't play ball, just grill the burgers indoors!

Devilish

Garlic has been regarded as a cure-all since Greek and Roman times. In the Middle Ages, it was even used against the plague and to cure those were possessed by the Devil!

I'm a man. Men cook outside. Women make the three-bean salad. That's the way it is and always has been...
(William Geist)

BBQ LAMBURGER

THESE SPICY BURGERS ARE SENSATIONAL AT A SUMMER BARBECUE, OR COOK THEM ANY TIME FOR A DELICIOUS FAMILY SUPPER. LAMB-TASTIC!

Serves 4

What to buy

* 1 lb ground lamb
* 1 egg
* 1 large onion, chopped
* 2 garlic cloves, crushed
* 2 tsp ground cumin
* 1 tsp ground coriander
* 1 tbsp paprika
* A handful of fresh flat-leaf parsley, chopped
* 1–2 handfuls of fresh breadcrumbs
* Salt and pepper
* 4 tbsp vegetable oil

How to cook it...

1 In a large bowl, knead together the lamb, egg, onion, and garlic with the cumin, coriander, paprika, and parsley. Add sufficient breadcrumbs to make the mixture easy to shape; knead them into the mixture. Season to taste.

2 Take one handful of the mixture at a time and shape into large burger patties. Set aside on a plate.

3 Place the burgers on the grill or under a hot broiler, then cook for about 10 minutes on both sides, or until done. Remove and drain on paper towels.

4 Serve with a salad or on burger buns, with a tray of your favorite dee-lish relishes.

Tuna for Health

Tuna—like most other fish—contains zinc. This miracle mineral ensures a healthy immune system and growth in children and adults. It also helps in cases of impotence or poor sex drive—and thus makes many people VERY happy!!!

I brought you a tuna sandwich. They say it's brain food. I guess because there's so much dolphin in it and you know how smart they are...
(Marge Simpson)

TUTTI FRUTTI TUNA

THIS JUICY, FRUITY, FISHY FEAST WILL GIVE YOU ZING AND ZEST FOR A WHOLE DAY—AND IT'S JUST SO EASY TO MAKE!

Serves 2

What to buy

* ❋ **2 tuna steaks**
* ❋ **7 oz can apricots, drained, with 2 tbsp of the syrup reserved**
* ❋ **2 tbsp dijon mustard**
* ❋ **1 tbsp lemon juice**
* ❋ **A piece fresh ginger, grated**
* ❋ **2 tbsp vegetable oil**

How to cook it...

1 Wash the tuna steaks and pat them dry with paper towels. Chop the apricots, place in a bowl with the reserved syrup, and combine with the mustard, lemon juice, and ginger. Place the tuna steaks in the marinade and turn to coat all over. Chill for 1 hour or longer.

2 Heat the oil in a large frying pan. Remove the tuna steaks from the marinade and pat dry. Discard the marinade. When the oil is hot, saute the steaks for 2-5 minutes on each side, or until just done and still pink in the center.

3 Transfer the tuna to serving plates, and serve with plenty of crusty bread.

Turkey is one of the best gifts that the New World has made to the Old...
(A. Brillat-Savarin)

Indian Chicken?

The turkey was already domesticated in Mexico at the time of the Aztecs, and one of the national dishes in Mexico is turkey with a sauce containing chocolate (*mole poblano de guajolote*). When the Spanish conquistadors arrived, they called turkeys "Indian chicken" because they still thought they were in India!

Some like it Hot

If you're happiest with hot flavors, pep up your turkey patties by mixing in ½ tsp chili powder and half a finely chopped red pepper. For a Middle Eastern taste, try adding ½ tsp ground cumin and ½ tsp ground coriander.

SMOKEY TURKEY PATTIES

THESE FEEL-GOOD PATTIES ARE A SWELL WAY TO USE UP YOUR LEFTOVER TURKEY FROM CHRISTMAS OR THANKSGIVING—AND TASTY TOO!

Makes 16

What to buy

* 2 ¼ lb cooked turkey
* 1 lb cooked potatoes, mashed
* 1 cup turkey gravy
* 2 tsp tomato purée
* Salt and pepper
* Fine dry breadcrumbs
* 2 tbsp vegetable oil
* Smoky barbecue sauce

How to cook it...

1 Grind the turkey or chop finely in a food processor. In a large bowl, combine the turkey with the mashed potato, gravy, and tomato purée. Season to taste, and shape into 16 flat patties.

2 Place the breadcrumbs on a large plate, and roll each burger in the breadcrumbs.

3 Heat the oil in a large frying pan. Fry the patties in batches, for about 5 minutes on each side, or until golden-brown and crisp. Pat dry with paper towels.

4 Serve the turkey patties as TV dinners, on a tray with the barbecue sauce, and a salad. Tune into your favorite show.

A spoonful of sugar

helps the medicine

go down...

Chapter Four

HELLO SUNSHINE!

Check out these Desserts and you'll be on Top of the World!

Nothing is more guaranteed to make you feel good than a delicious dessert!

CONTENTS

Hello Sunshine!

CHOCOHOLIC'S DREAM DESSERT

INDULDGE YOUR SECRET PASSION WITH THIS CREAMY DESSERT—IT'S IRRESISTIBLE, SO WHY FIGHT IT?

Serves 4

What to buy

※ 8 oz unsweetened chocolate, broken into pieces

※ 1 tbsp orange liqueur

※ 4 oz butter, softened

※ 4 oz superfine granulated sugar

※ 4 eggs, separated

※ 5 fl oz whipping cream

※ A few drops of vanilla flavoring

How to make it...

1 Put the chocolate into a bowl with 2 tbsp water and the liqueur. Place over a pan of simmering water and stir until melted and smooth. Cool slightly.

2 Beat the butter with the sugar until pale and fluffy. Beat in the egg yolks, one at a time.

3 Add the chocolate to the butter mixture and beat for 5 minutes.

4 Whisk the egg whites until stiff, but not dry, and fold them into the chocolate mixture. Spoon into individual cups and chill until set.

5 Whip the cream and stir in the vanilla flavoring. Serve with cookies, and a coffee liqueur for extra happiness measures.

Laughter is brightest
where food is best...
(Irish Proverb)

Versatile Fruit

Cranberries are high in vitamin C but very low in
calories: they are almost 90 percent water, and thus
will definitely not pile on the pounds. Often served
with turkey or game, they have a long history of
association with meat. Native Americans pounded
cranberries into a paste and mixed this with dried
meat; a mixture they called "pemmican."

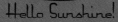
Hello Sunshine!

CRANBERRY CRIMBO CRUMBLE

HAVE A MERRY, BERRY CHRISTMAS WITH THIS FANTASTIC FESTIVE BAKE!

Serves 4

What to buy

* 1 oz ready-to-eat packet dried cranberries
* Zest and juice of 1 large orange
* 5 oz all-purpose flour
* 4 oz butter, chilled and diced
* 3 oz superfine granulated sugar
* 1 oz chopped almonds
* ½ tsp ground allspice
* 14 oz can mango slices in syrup, drained
* Vanilla custard, to serve

How to cook it...

1 Heat the oven to 375°F.

2 Place the cranberries and orange juice in a small pan and bring to a boil; remove from the heat and set aside for 5 minutes.

3 Meanwhile, place the flour and butter in a large bowl, and rub together with your fingers until the mixture resembles coarse breadcrumbs. Stir in the sugar, almonds, and mixed spice.

4 Combine the cranberries and orange juice with the mango and the zest. Spoon the mixture into a buttered pie dish and sprinkle over the crumble. Bake in the oven for 25–30 minutes until golden brown.

5 Serve with hot vanilla custard and get festive!

POMEGRANATE WONDER ICE

THIS SENSATIONAL ICE IS PERFECT AT THE END OF ANY MEAL

Serves 4

What to buy

* 4 pomegranates
* 4 oz superfine granulated sugar
* 2 tbsp lemon juice
* 2 tsp grenadine syrup

How to cook it...

1 Halve the pomegranates and spoon out the juice and seeds. Press through a fine sieve, to squeeze out. Place in a bowl and stir in the sugar, lemon juice, and grenadine. Stir until the sugar has dissolved.

2 Pour the fruit mixture into a flat-based, rectangular freezer container. Cover and place in the freezer.

3 After about 1–1 ½ hours, remove from the freezer. Whisk to beat the frozen edges back into the mixture and turn it into a slush; return to the freezer.

4 Repeat this process twice, each time leaving the sorbet to partially freeze before removing it

from the freezer, then whisking the frozen bits back into the mixture.

5 Finally, allow at least another hour of further freezing before serving the pomegranate wonder ice—that's if you can keep everyone away from the freezer!

Cooking is not chemistry. It is an art. It requires instinct and taste rather than exact measurements...

(Marcel Boulestin)

Fertile Fruit

The pomegranate is one of the oldest fruits in cultivation. Much favored as a symbol of fertility, there are references to these fruits in both the Bible and the Koran. Today, pomegranates are mainly prized for their deliciously delicate flavor.

Potent Potassium

Bananas are especially high in potassium. This mineral is responsible for transporting oxygen to the brain. It also gives us more energy and prevents high blood pressure. What a good excuse to eat these muffins!

All-American

Americans are renowned for their baking, and the muffin is one of their greatest exports. There is also a British version of the muffin, but it is not as light and definitely not as easy to make as its American cousin. Today there are thousands of recipes with dozens of different ingredients, ranging from chocolate to coffee, from blueberries to apricots, and from pecans to walnuts.

The only way to get rid of a temptation is to yield to it... (Oscar Wilde)

GRANNY'S NANA MUFFINS

ALL THESE MUFFINS NEED IS A DOLLOP OF CREAM TO SET THEM OFF TO PERFECTION. GRANNY REALLY DOES KNOW BEST!

Makes 20 muffins

What to buy

* **2 oz butter**
* **1 ½ tbsp superfine granulated sugar**
* **1 egg, lightly beaten**
* **3 fl oz milk**
* **1 tsp cinnamon**
* **5 oz all-purpose flour**
* **½ tsp baking powder**
* **A pinch of salt**
* **½ banana, finely chopped**
* **A handful of blueberries (if available)**
* **2 oz pecans, finely chopped**
* **Brown sugar, to coat**

How to cook it...

1 Heat the oven to 400°F. In a bowl, whisk the butter and sugar together until soft, then fold in the egg, milk, and cinnamon.

2. Add the flour, baking powder, and salt to the mixture. Gently fold in, using a metal spoon in a figure of eight. Do not stir. Gently fold in the banana, blueberries, and the nuts.

3 Spoon the mixture into muffin cups. Sprinkle with the sugar and bake for 20 minutes, or until the muffins have risen and turned brown. Take out and place on a wire rack to cool.

4 Serve hot or cold—with a generous helping of cream. Yum!

Cold Date

According to the Diaphoenix Electuary, the "date purges the pituitary of the serosities of the brain," which means that it is good for a cold. Dates were indeed used as a cold remedy by the Arabs and in the Middle Ages, and in the Near East some astonishing 365 culinary and pharmaceutical uses were listed for this wonder fruit!

Pick a Date

Fresh dates are now widely available in winter. Deliciously soft and sweet, you should eat them quickly as they can go sour. Dried dates, unlike many other dried fruits, are not treated with sulfur, so they're better for you!

O thou, thou red, thou date! Neither the fig nor the grape can compare with thee... (Date-Sellers in Cairo)

Hello Sunshine!

DATE-A-PUDDING

A FEEL-GOOD DESSERT THAT'S FULL OF FRUITY FLAVOR—COULD IT BE THE
PERFECT PUDDING FOR YOUR DATE?

Serves 4

What to buy

* **5 tbsp whole white rice**
* **5 dates, chopped**
* **2 oz superfine granulated sugar**
* **3 3/4 cups milk**
* **1/2 oz butter**
* **Light cream or Greek-style yogurt to serve**

How to cook it...

1 Heat the oven to 300°F. In a bowl, combine the rice, chopped dates, and sugar with the milk, then pour into a lightly buttered, ovenproof dish (about 2 pints). Cut the butter into small pieces and dot over the rice mixture.

2 Bake for 2 hours in the oven, stirring every 30 minutes, until the rice is tender.

3 Serve immediately, with a drizzle of light cream, or a spoonful of Greek-style yogurt and honey.

APPETIZING APPLE TARTLETS

HEAVENLY TARTS STRAIGHT FROM PARADISE—AND WHO CARES ABOUT THE CALORIES?

Serves 4

What to buy

✳ **5 oz white marzipan, cut into small pieces**

✳ **5 tbsp heavy cream**

✳ **2 oz roasted hazelnuts, roughly chopped**

✳ **11-oz pack ready-rolled puff pastry**

✳ **2 eating apples, cored and thinly sliced**

✳ **1 oz superfine granulated sugar**

✳ **A little butter**

✳ **1 tbsp apricot jam**

How to cook it...

1 Heat the oven to 400°F. Place the marzipan, cream, and the chopped hazelnuts into a food processor and process to a thick paste.

2 Unroll the pastry and spread the marzipan-nut paste thinly over the top. Cut out 8 rounds, using a saucer or a 4 in cutter, then transfer to a baking sheet.

3 Arrange the apple slices in a wheel-pattern over each pastry circle. Dot a little butter on the apple and sprinkle with the superfine granulated sugar. Bake in the oven for about 15 minutes, or until risen and golden.

4 Meanwhile put the apricot jam into a small saucepan together with 3 tbsp water and heat gently until the jam has melted, stirring occasionally. Make sure the jam does not burn.

5 Sieve the jam and then brush over each tart, using a pastry brush or the back of a teaspoon.

6 Serve the tartlets with a glass of sweet dessert wine to make this a perfect day.

Comfort me with apples: for I am sick of love... (The Song of Solomon 2:4)

More Apples

Our eating and shopping habits have reduced the number of different apple varieties that are commercially available from a potential 7,000 to only about 100, and of these just eight varieties make up the most popular ones. So if you want to see more than just Golden Delicious and Granny Smith in your shop, seek out some unusual varieties from small growers.

TIPSY PINEAPPLE TREATS

IT DOESN'T TAKE MUCH TO SPREAD A LITTLE HAPPINESS—JUST FOUR INGREDIENTS WILL DO!

Serves 4

What to buy

* 1 large pineapple
* 4 tbsp dark soft brown sugar
* 1 oz butter
* 4 tbsp rum

How to cook it...

1 Quarter the pineapple lengthways, slicing through the leafy crown. Using a sharp knife, cut out the central core from each quarter, then cut between the flesh and the skin. Free the flesh completely, but leave it in position. Cut the flesh in half lengthwise and then across into bite-size pieces.

2 Heat the grill. Place the pineapple quarters in a grill pan and sprinkle each one with 1 tbsp sugar. Cut the butter into small pieces and dot evenly over the pineapple.

3 Broil at high heat for 4-5 minutes until the pineapple is heated through and the sugar has dissolved. Transfer to serving dishes.

4 Gently heat the rum in a small saucepan over a low heat. Remove from the heat and set alight in the pan. (You may want to do this in front of the other diners—it's quite spectacular!) As soon as the flames have died down, pour over the pineapple quarters.

5 Serve at once and watch everyone's eyes light up with a sudden rush of happiness!

A (pine)apple
a day keeps the
doctor away...
(After the
folk Saying)

Bon Appetit!

Pineapples contain an amazing enzyme called bromelain. In cooking this enzyme is used for tenderizing meat, but it also has medicinal value: pineapples aid digestion, relieve stomach upsets, and give you back a healthy appetite for food. Bromelain is also widely used in skin care products—so perhaps we should speak of a pineapple, rather than a peach, complexion.

Hello Sunshine!

MARVELOUSLY LIMEY MERINGUE PIE

CRUNCHY, STICKY, AND CREAMY, THIS SURE IS A DELIGHTFUL DESSERT.

Serves 4

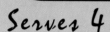

What to buy

- ✳ 6 oz frozen short-crust (unsweetened) pastry, defrosted
- ✳ 1 ½ oz cornstarch
- ✳ Juice and grated zest of 2 limes
- ✳ 3 oz sugar
- ✳ 2 large eggs, separated
- ✳ A pinch of salt
- ✳ 4 oz superfine granulated sugar

How to cook it...

1 Heat the oven to 400°F. Line a 7-inch baking pan with the pastry, prick the base thoroughly, and bake for 15 minutes. Remove from the oven and lower the heat to 300°F.

2 Measure ½ pt water. Blend the cornstarch to a smooth paste with a little of it. Heat the remaining water with the lime juice and zest, then stir in the cornstarch paste and bring to a boil, stirring continuously.

3 Simmer for 2 minutes. Remove from the heat and stir in sugar and egg yolks. Cool slightly, then pour into the pastry case.

4 Beat the egg whites, salt, and sugar until stiff. Spread over the filling, making sure the mixture meets the pastry edge, then make peaks with a spoon.

5. Bake for 35–40 minutes, until the meringue is crisp and golden, and ready to be devoured!

Try Thai

Limes are great fruit to use in Thai meals––they combine really well with fresh cilantro, garlic, and chili. If you just need a small amount of juice, push a sharp knife into the fruit and squeeze out what you need.

Fresh Breath

Apart from its well-known properties as a preventor of scurvy, the lime also has a more unusual use: like alcohol and green tea, this citrus fruit is particularly well-suited for freshening the mouth. So, between courses, rather than having a cigarette, bite into a slice of lime!

POLLY'S PEACHY TARTS

PEACHES AND CREAM ARE A MARRIAGE MADE IN HEAVEN. HERE'S THE PERFECT OUTCOME OF THE UNION!

Makes 4-6

What to buy

* ½ oz butter
* 8 oz frozen puff pastry, thawed
* 1 lb peaches
* 2 tbsp superfine granulated sugar
* Freshly grated nutmeg
* Lightly whipped cream

How to cook it...

1 Butter a large baking sheet and sprinkle with a little water.

2 On a floured surface, roll out the defrosted puff pastry to a large rectangle, about 16 x 10 inches, and cut into four or six small rectangles.

3 Transfer the rectangles to the baking sheet. Using the back of a small knife, shape the edges of the pastry. Then, using the tip of the knife, score a line about a half-an-inch from the edge of each rectangle to form a border. Heat the oven to 400°F.

4 Cut the peaches in half and remove the pits, then slice the fruit thinly. Arrange the peach slices down the center of the rectangles, leaving

the border on each side uncovered. Sprinkle with the sugar and a little nutmeg.

5 Bake for 12-15 minutes in the oven, or until the edges of the pastry are nicely puffed and the fruit is tender. Transfer the tarts to a wire rack to cool.

6 Serve with dollops of whipped cream, and cups of strong black coffee.

An apple is an excellent thing— until you have tried a peach... (George du Maurier)

Ever Hopeful

The blossoming of the peach trees is eagerly awaited in Japan and China each year as a sign of the arrival of spring, the season of renewal and growth. Brides wear peach blossom wreaths—symbolizing their virginity and promising many children.

DEVILISHLY DELICIOUS CHOCOLATE CAKE

GO ON, BE A DEVIL AND RUSTLE UP THIS WICKED CHOCOLATE CAKE.

Serves 8

What to buy

* 4 oz fresh cherries
* 3 tbsp brandy
* 1 lb unsweetened chocolate
* 7 oz butter
* 3 eggs, separated, plus 3 egg yolks
* 4 oz brown sugar
* 3 oz self-rising flour
* 2 oz ground almonds
* 6 tbsp light cream

How to cook it...

1 Pit half the cherries and soak them in the brandy for at least 1 hour.

2 Heat the oven to 350°F. Grease and line an 8-inch round deep cake pan with wax paper. Drain the cherries, reserving the brandy. Break the chocolate into small pieces and melt half of it, together with 4 oz of the butter, in a bowl set over a pan containing boiling water. Allow to cool slightly.

3 In a separate bowl, whisk the egg yolks and sugar until light and fluffy. Add the melted chocolate and brandy and mix. Fold in the flour, ground almonds, and soaked cherries. Whisk the egg whites until stiff, then gently fold into the chocolate. Spoon into the pan and smooth

the top. Bake for 40 minutes. Transfer the cake
to a wire rack and leave to cool.

4 Melt the remaining chocolate and the cream
in a bowl set over a pan containing boiling
water. Take off the heat. Beat in the remaining
butter and egg yolks until smooth. Chill until
thickened.

5 Cut the cake in half and spread two-thirds
of the filling on the bottom half, then sandwich
together again and spread the remaining
mixture over the top. Decorate the cake with
the remaining cherries.

6 Serve as a grand finale to a happy meal—
and make sure you get one of the pieces with
a cherry on top!

Mayan Gold

**When a Spanish conquistador arrived in
Mexico, looking for gold, he found chocolate—
and soon discovered its aphrodisiac as well as
money-making potential!**

Once in a while
I say, "Go for
it," and I eat
chocolate...
(Claudia
Schiffer)